Fiverr Freedom

From Your First Gig To Making A Fortune On Fiverr

Brad Jones

Copyright © 2015 HRD Publishing

ISBN-13: 978-1515262381
ISBN-10: 1515262383

CONTENTS

INTRODUCTION

So you are thinking about starting a business on Fiverr.com?

Fiverr is a great website to get your break into the freelancing world and leave your 9-5 job behind for good! Many have done it already, so why can't you be the next?

This book gives you all the in's and out's you need to become a successful, Top Rated Seller on Fiverr. Generate as little or as much income as you want and get rewarded by gaining levels, experience and a superior self-esteem boost when the positive reviews start flooding in!

If you have been thinking for ages about starting a business, freelancing or just quitting your job to do something you love, then Fiverr could be just what you were looking for to get your foot in the door and your ideas off the ground!

No matter how skilled you are or aren't, there is a gig out there that you are meant to be selling!

Don't waste time, learn what it takes to become a Fiverr Super Seller, take action from what you learn in this book and leave that boring desk job behind for good!

WHAT IS FIVERR AND WHY SHOULD I USE IT?

What is Fiverr?

To put it simply, Fiverr.com is the world's very first marketplace for services as a product. Buying a service like logo design, article writing or website creation has never been easier than with Fiverr's unique system.

How does it work?

Just like a shopper on Amazon would search the product they are looking for, Fiverr allows you to search, review and order almost any service you could think of from a number of different sellers around the world.

Fiverr's services are known as "gigs" and each and every gig starts off selling at $5. These gigs are then categorized into different niches, such as Writing and Translation, Graphics and Design, Music and Audio and there is even one titled Fun and Bizarre.

From those categories they are separated further into sub-categories to keep it neat and organized. The gigs displayed are generally sellers who have high ratings for the service you are searching.

Can Fiverr make you real money?

As a seller, you must always offer a service for $5. That amount might not get you too excited, but you can add what are called "gig extra's" and this is where the REAL money is made. Gig extra's allow you to tack on a higher price tag by offering an additional service.

For example, someone's gig may be to write 500 words for $5. An extra for this service could be "I will write an additional 1500 words for $20". Another gig extra in this example could be "I will write 500 words in 24 hours for $10". When someone purchases 2000 words or a 24 hour turnaround, the order would then cost $25 or $15 instead of $5.

7

When you start getting multiple orders, all with gig extra's attached, the money starts to add up pretty quick. If you have excellent customer service and have over a 97% positive rating, then you are almost guaranteed to be high in the search ranks and easily found over other users.

The biggest concern you have, is getting your account to that Level Two or Top Rated Seller status as smoothly as possible. Just like on Amazon, customers with a bad experience can leave a bad review. Bad review's hurt your rating more than you could possibly imagine when you are a new seller. Coming back from those bad reviews can be even more difficult. Success on Fiverr is not down to the quantity of gigs you do. It's all about offering a high quality service. Once you're able to offer a quality service, the quantity of gigs will follow.

What does Fiverr get out of it?

Of course, there is no way something this grand could come without some sort of price tag! While memberships on Fiverr.com are free, Fiverr does charge the buyer a $0.50 processing fee and the sellers a 20% of each sale, ($1 of every $5) basically for being the middle man, so to speak.

How do you know you will get paid?

Payments are made immediately when a buyer places an order. The order appears in the sellers To-Do list and the seller has a specified timeframe to complete the order (which the seller sets when the gig is created). Once the seller delivers the order and the buyer has left a review, it will show how much you have earned.

However, this money is not available immediately. There is a 14 day clearing period between the completion of the gig and when you can withdraw you funds from Fiverr.com.

How do I get my money?

To receive your revenues on Fiverr you can go one of two routes. You can use a PayPal account, or you can apply to receive a Fiverr Payoneer prepaid debit card. Both have their own fees associated with different transactions and only you can decide which of these options is right for you. Just be sure you read everything, especially with regards to fees, with both payment options before making your decision.

Why Fiverr is the Best Site for Freelancers

The marketplace for services as a product is a revelation in the world of freelancing. It has never before been easier to be a seller of a service. You don't go out looking for all the contracts yourself and you don't have to compete with 45 other people for one gig. You offer a service and someone who needs that service can order it with the click of a button. It really is that simple!

If you have ever considered venturing outside that 9-5 desk job or the odd hours of working retail and restaurants for the chance to be your own boss, Fiverr is a great way to get there! Many people have done it already and more and more are joining them each year. I'm going to share stories of three people that have done just that later in this book.

The Fiverr blog is filled with posts about Fiverr Super Seller's, who are sellers on Fiverr who have been recognized for their success and were granted Top Rated Seller status. Some, if not all of these sellers are full-time Fiverr sellers now. They have accomplished things like saving for vacations or buying a house, so what's stopping you from doing it too?

At the end of each chapter in this book I'll list a set of actions for you to take to make sure you're taking steps towards Fiverr success.

Actions from this chapter

- Set up a Fiverr account with an associated Paypal account or Fiverr Payoneer prepaid debit card.

- List three Goals you want from working on Fiverr. Write them down, tell at least one person about them and display them somewhere you'll see them everyday. How much do you want to make a month on Fiverr? Or do you want to become a Top Rated Seller in 12 months?

STARTING OUT – PROFILE AND GIG CREATION

How to set up an exceptional profile

The first and foremost important part of starting your business on Fiverr is to create a unique and enticing profile. Make yourself someone people will want to work with. Everything from your profile picture to your grammar and spelling are to be taken very seriously in the creation of your profile and gigs.

Before you start creating your own profile, check out some of the Top Rated Seller and Level Two Seller profiles for ideas, especially the ones in the same field you're looking to do gigs in. Try to give off the same professional and personal impression that they provide. How do they structure their sentences? How do they make their gig appealing to you? It's a useful exercise to look at least five profiles from Top Rated Sellers, and make notes on what you like on each one. You're likely to find some similarities between them. This research should help you understand what an appealing profile looks like, which is very useful when you're about to make your own.

One of the biggest factors in creating your profile is to have a professional picture of yourself. Having a head shot of yourself rather than a logo or group photo can create a more human and personal experience for the buyer. Even though the services are being paid for and delivered in an electronic form, it is still comforting to know they are working with a real person. Which profile pictures from your research of Top Rated Sellers stood out to you? Why have they stood out? How can you replicate what they've done and have a stand out profile picture too?

After you have chosen a professional profile picture it is time to write your "about" section. There are a few really important things you need to do here. You need to project a professional image of yourself in a very small amount of words first of all.

Fiverr really does not give you much space to talk about yourself and you will not be putting a portfolio up with samples of previous work or a job history. So without the aid of credentials and proven experience, you have to convince your customers that they should pick you over anyone else, all in very few words.

If you are an expert in your industry such as graphic design or writing, then say so. If you have 10 years of experience, then let your buyers know! Just make sure you are honest and you have the skills to back it up. If you are selling a service that is new to you, think about whether or not you have any related experience to mention.

Once you have decided what you are going to say, you will want to make sure that you triple check all your spelling and grammar. This step is super important because a poorly written profile can absolutely drive traffic to another seller. No matter what you are planning to sell, a well written profile will put you a step above a lot of the competition.

The last concern when writing your little 'about you' blurb is going to be that you not only sound professional and have great spelling and grammar, but also to be as friendly and inviting as possible. Until you have buyers who leave positive feedback, this will be the only way to entice your buyers to choose you over the other couple thousand people selling the same or similar service. Use your research once again to highlight the "about" sections that stood out to you as a potential buyer.

Here is an example of a great "about" section to get you started:

"I am a Graphic Designer and Photographer with several years of experience in the Adobe Creative Suite. I am passionate about creating quality images and designs for individuals and companies. I enjoy working in Photoshop and Lightroom to edit and manipulate images or photograph local wildlife in my spare time. I will provide you with quality designs or photos for a number of different needs, so message me today! I look forward to working with you!"

Once you have a professional profile picture of yourself and a well written, to the point, friendly and inviting 'about you' blurb, the only thing left to complete your profile is to verify your social media. Even though all communications about Fiverr orders must be made through Fiverr (read their Terms of Service) they still ask you to verify your Facebook account, Google+ account and your e-mail address.

If you have done all of this, it is time to move on to creating your first gig!

Creating the Perfect Money-Maker

Now that it is time to create your first gig, you need to decide one important thing: What is $5 worth to you? This question is so important because you do not want to choose a gig that will have you investing 2 or 3 hours for $5 as that is simply not profitable.

Another aspect to consider is even if you can do something in 15 minutes, is this because you are highly skilled and experienced in this area? Is this something that would normally cost extra? If it is, then dial it back just a little. You want to leave room to make more with Gig Extra's.

Make sure you choose something that you know you can deliver with quality every single time. This is important because every customer will have the opportunity to leave feedback and negative feedback early on will cause a much longer road to success.

If you're unsure what you can offer, spend some time reviewing the sites current gigs. Can you find any gigs that you could do for $5? If you're still struggling to find something, spend some time looking through the 'More' job section, and look through the current gigs on 'Fun & Bizarre' and 'Other'. Not only is it entertaining, but it should get your creative juices flowing. There are so many weird and wonderful gigs out there that people are paying for. There are very few limits. I would encourage you to stop putting up barriers as to why you can't do the gigs that they're doing, and start asking yourself "why not?!".

After you decide what service you will offer for your base $5 gig, you need to come up with a catchy title. All gig titles are displayed as "I will (insert catchy title here) for $5". Choosing a brilliant title for your gig is almost as important as the service itself.

Now it is time to sell your skills. While the "about" section in your profile is very limited, they give you a pretty decent amount of space to work with in your gig description.

Your gig description is a vital part of selling your gig. This is what will be displayed when a buyer searches, finds and clicks on your gig and this is how they will know what to expect from you. Be specific, make sure you outline for the buyer exactly what you will provide for them with a single $5 gig.

This will help immensely when customers go to order and will help cut down on the need for cancellations if someone orders expecting your service to be something else.

After you have a killer description written up (once again, perfect spelling and grammar will put you miles above a lot of gigs), you will want to choose pictures to represent your gig. Choose an image that properly represents the service you are selling.

For example, a logo design gig is one where you can use samples of your own work while providing proper image(s) for your service.

Another great option at your disposal to drive traffic to your gig is to add a video. Creating a short video of yourself explaining your services is a great way to bring in orders. This is the perfect way to show people the real you and they are likely to choose you over someone else for that reason alone.

On top of all this you will want to optimize your keywords. Choose the most relevant terms to your gig. Your keywords are vital to making sure that people searching your services will find you.

As an example, your gig is logo design so keywords could be "logo design", "graphic design", "logos", "graphics".

The final step before publishing and activating your gig is to choose how many days it will take you to deliver. When someone places an order, there will be a count-down clock on the order page and the limit is however many days you selected for delivery. Make sure that you choose a reasonable timeframe for the type of work you are selling and your own schedule. Find a balance in offering a reasonable turnaround time whilst not putting yourself under too much pressure.

As you build up your profile, collect reviews and grow as a seller you will need to tweak your profile and gig description as necessary. If you find that people are constantly asking you for a service you do not provide, consider adding it as a Gig Extra or separate Gig later on. Continue to check the profiles, and gig listings from the Top Rated Sellers in your niche.

Some of the best tips can be found on the Fiverr Forum so be sure to comb through those right from the get-go. The Fiverr community is a group of people who all really want to help one another succeed in the common goal of being your own boss.

Actions from this chapter

- Look at 5 Top Rated Seller Profiles and make notes on what you like.

- Complete your Fiverr Profile – Professional Photo and 'About' Section.

- Check out the Fiverr Forum and read at least 3 Posts. This will show you how useful it is and demonstrate how you can use it to help your business succeed.

BEST SELLING GIGS

If you plan on making a living through Fiverr or at least a considerable amount of money, you'll need to find the best selling gigs for you. There is no 'special secret' niche that will make you more money than the rest. It comes down to knowing what service you can offer at a high level, consistently. That's it. Easy right!

The only way you're going to turn your Fiverr account into a business, is if you're able to replicate something that's worth more money, consistently, over a long period of time. Consider what gig's you would enjoy doing most. What are your passions and hobbies in life? Fiverr can allow you to get paid for doing something you love. Take that opportunity!

If you're getting paid to do something you love, it no longer feels like work. Its fun, and you'll continue to do more of it. Before you know it, you'll be making a lot of money very easily.

Try different gigs out. Make a note of which ones were quick to complete, fun to do, and had the most potential for Gig extras.

Getting Started

Simple is better when you are starting out. If you are not exactly sure what experience you have to offer then these are a few "easy" gig's to consider:

o I will test your website from a user's point of view for $5

o I will tweet your message to (###) of REAL followers on Twitter for $5

o I will model your merchandise or hold your sign for $5

None of these things are particularly difficult to do. Testing out a website is simple, just give your opinion on design as far as layout and graphics, make sure all the links work, etc. Then let the website owner know what is great and what could use improvement from a user's point of view.

Tweeting a message out about someone else's product or service is a great advertising technique for many industries. If you already have a large following on Twitter, then why not utilize that as a way to make money with advertising?

Modeling merchandise or holding a sign with a logo or message is a great, easy way to make a few bucks. People can use this for magazines or website content. Pet models also have gigs like this if you are too shy to get on camera yourself!

 If you are a looking for something just a little more advanced, consider these options:

- o   I will write a (###) word blog post or article for $5

- o   I will design a custom Facebook page for $5

- o   I will promote your product or service on my blog for $5

Writing a blog post or article can be either very easy or very difficult. If you are a great writer and researching topics is a breeze for you, then this could be very lucrative. If you know you can get this done in under half an hour you've done well for the price you charge.

If you are good with social media, then maybe you can charge for creating someone's business or event page? If you have the know-how and someone else doesn't, then why not sell it as a service on Fiverr.

Just like the Twitter gig in the easier set, you can offer to promote services and products on your personal blog if you have a decent following. This gig is only a little more difficult in the fact that instead of a short tweet, a full blog post is required for a blog mention.

If you know you have experience in a niche that is a little more advanced, you might offer gigs like these:

- o   I will design a professional t-shirt for $5

- o   I will record a professional voice over in any accent for $5

- o   I will make an animated animal that will speak your message for $5

T-shirt designs are a little more involved and as with any graphic design job can be done in several different ways. How you go about this gig would be up to your own individual skills and comfort zone, but it is sure to be a great selling gig.

Voice over work is incredibly profitable. Those who can manipulate their voice in a unique way are destined for this profession and there are dozens of great voices out there. If you often find yourself doing impressions – and rather good ones at that – then this could be the gig for you to try.

Combining both of those talents is even more impressive. Animating an animal or object, creating any sort of video, is definitely a bit of work for any designer. Adding on the fact that you can add your voice over talent to that to speak a designated message will make your animation all the more appealing.

These are all merely suggestions to think over. What skill level you feel you are comfortable in and what sort of gig you sell is completely up to you in the end. Getting ideas from featured or top selling gigs is a great way to find inspiration, but never copy their gig exactly. Find a way to make what you sell unique from the rest.

Like instead of saying:

"I will design a professional logo for $5"

Try something like this:

"I will create a unique and artistic logo for $5"

Or

"I will design a memorable and marketable logo for $5"

Try to think about what you can do to deliver a unique product for a great price. It's all about standing out in the crowd after you find that perfect gig.

Be Patient

You might not find the best selling gig for you in the first couple of months. Keep experimenting and evaluating your experience to date. You will start to realize which gigs make you more money, faster, and give you the most pleasure completing. Stick to your Fiverr Goals, persevere, and Fiverr success will come.

Be Flexible

Don't restrict your options when it comes to offering a gig. Try something new and see how you get on. The more options you have to start with, the more likely you're going to find a route to success. If you only offer one Gig you have to make sure it's a success to make it on Fiverr, there's no back up. But, if you offer out five Gigs, you can afford to fail on 80% of them and become a success on the one option. That's all it takes. Can you think of 10 or 20 Gigs?

Actions from this chapter

- Make a list of at least 5 Gigs you could do on Fiverr – Consider which one's you could add the most Gig extras to, which one's you're most experienced in, and which one's would be the most enjoyable to do.

- Create your first Gig. You've done plenty of note taking, researching and thinking. Now it's time to make some money!

- Extend your list of 5 potential Gigs to 10 or 20.

- Keep track of how much you make from each Gig niche and how many jobs you've completed. By recording this information you can see which Gig's give you the biggest bang for your buck, and which one's are the most popular.

EARN LEVELS AND SELL MORE WITH GREAT CUSTOMER SERVICE

Once you have got your first customer it's time to prove your skills and show them what you've got. It's not just about your skills directly tied to the work you are doing though. Just like any other business, customer service is first and foremost important. You could give them the best logo, website design or article they have ever seen but they are not likely to leave a good review or work with you again if they received bad customer service.

You want every customer to feel like they are your number one client.

Answer them promptly (this will also keep your responsiveness time down – which is displayed on your profile!) and make sure that you secure all details needed for the assignment before you ever start working. This will ensure that the project is delivered on time and with quality.

If possible, finish the work early and send it in for them to view. If they are happy with it, then deliver. If they asked for a few revisions, then you have just guaranteed that it will be right on delivery. This is a great tactic to avoid the buyer asking for modifications after you deliver – which will prolong you getting paid!

Great customer service is simple to provide, all you have to do is be polite and be sure to cover all the buyers' needs from the start. Ask questions if you are not sure about something – it is better to know rather than guess and have to re-do a ton of work.

Be sure to keep the buyer updated – if you had a power-outage or family emergency and fell behind because of it, let your buyer know. Most of the time they will be happy to wait the extra day, especially if you made sure to let them know A.S.A.P. Downloading the Fiverr App is a great way to keep in contact with your customers no matter what happens.

If you are consistent with your customer service skills and always deliver a quality product on time, then you should have no problem gaining enough reviews to move up to Level One and soon after all the way to Top Rated Seller.

Though remember, no matter how great you are, there will always be troubling buyers. There might be people who just expect you to do hours of work and revisions for next to no money. There are a handful of buyers who expect that everything cost $5, no matter what the service being provided and that simply is not true.

Great customer service absolutely does not mean that you have to do excessive amounts of extra work for free. This is extremely counterproductive as a seller and people may come to expect it out of you. Set your rates to be competitive and reasonable and never do work for free!

If someone asks you in a message to do work for them and let them order later then kindly tell them that you cannot do any work until the order has been placed. The worst that happens is they will go scam someone else instead of you – and the best that happens is they take the time and place the order.

How Do Levels Work?

As a New Seller you are a little limited, but in recent updates to the site they do give you more options to help increase sales and earn levels.

New Sellers Get:

- o   2 Gig Extras ($5, $10 and $20)

- o   5 Gig Multiples Available

- o   Extra Fast Delivery Option

With these options you are able to add up to 2 gig extras per gig up to $20, people can order up to 5 multiples of your gig at a time and you can even charge extra for Extra Fast delivery. (Extra Fast could be 24 hours or more depending on the original delivery time for your particular gig and can be different on each gig.)

To obtain Level One you need to:

- o Have an active account for a minimum of 30 days

- o Complete a minimum of 10 individual orders

- o Maintain a 4 star or above positive rating

- o Have a low cancellation rate

Now that you are a Level One Seller you have access to:

- o 4 Gig Extra's ($5, $10, $20 and $40)

- o 10 Gig Multiples Available

- o Extra Fast Delivery Option

- o Custom Offers (up to $1500)

- o Fiverr Anywhere

This gives you more room to make more money. With Fiverr Anywhere you are able to propose custom offers anywhere whether it be on Fiverr, Facebook or your personal blog. Custom quotes can also be made through messages when a customer comes to you with a project you can do but do not have a gig to cover.

To obtain Level Two you need to:

- o Complete a minimum of 50 individual orders within 2 consecutive months

- o Maintain a 4.5 star rating or higher

- o Have a low cancellation rate

Once you are Level Two you have access to:

5 Gig Extra's ($5, $10, $20, $40, $50)

- o   15 Gig Multiples Available

- o   Extra Fast Delivery Option

- o   Custom Offers

- o   Fiverr Anywhere

- o   Priority Customer Support

Once you have reached Level Two, you can consider yourself a highly successful Fiverr Seller. You have shown that your customer service is exemplary and you can deliver a quality product over and over again!

Now that you are a Level Two seller, it is time to reach for the stars and become a Top Rated Seller. This process is a little different than the other levels.

Top Rated Sellers are handpicked by Fiverr staff and the decision to be promoted to Top Rated Seller is based on many different criteria.

A Top Rated Seller is expected to have:

- o   A consistent 4.7 – 5 star rating

- o   Exceptional customer care

- o   Low cancellation rates

- o   Community leadership

- o   Decent volume of sales

Some have reached this goal in very little time while for others it may take a while. No matter how long it takes you, 3 months, a year or more, it is still a great honor to become a Top Rated Seller.

As a Top Rated Seller you will have these advantages available to you:

- o 6 Gig Extra's ($5, $10, $20, $40, $50, $100)

- o 20 Gig Multiples Available

- o Extra Fast Delivery Option

- o Fiverr Anywhere

- o Custom Offers

- o VIP Customer Support

Gaining levels is a great confidence booster and with every level you earn, you will be able to promote your sales in many different ways. Every Fiverr Seller should strive to become a Top Rated Seller, especially if they want to truly escape the 9-5 and be able to live off of an income from Fiverr.

Actions from this chapter

- Are you utilizing Gig extras? Remember this is the REAL money maker on Fiverr. If not, find other sellers in your niche and see what they're offering. Can you offer that too?

- Work towards a Level One Seller - Have an active account for a minimum of 30 days. Complete a minimum of 10 orders. Maintain a 4 star or above positive rating. Have a low cancellation rate.

- Update your Profile to highlight your experience and skills on Fiverr.

- Work towards a Level Two Seller - Complete a minimum of 50 individual orders within 2 consecutive months (25 a month, 6-7 a week). Maintain a 4.5 star rating or higher. Have a low cancellation rate.

- Update your Profile one again to highlight your experience and skills.

- Work towards a Top Rated Seller - Consistent 4.7-5.0 star rating. Exceptional customer care. Low cancellation rates. Community leadership. Decent volume of sales.

WATCH YOUR BUSINESS GROW

A lot of work is done for you already as far as finding buyers on Fiverr. That is not to say that you should never self-promote anyway! Just as with any business, self-promotion is a great way to expand your Fiverr business. You can have the best service in your niche on Fiverr, but if you're not getting the word out there how are people going to know about what you can do. You need to get some more exposure in order to take your Fiverr business to the next level.

Create a blog, Facebook page, Youtube channel or Twitter page. All of these options work. The more options you have, the better chance you have of success. Don't limit your options!

Once you have a dedicated page for your Fiverr gigs you are ready to start promoting.

Recommend to all your buyers that they like your pages and follow your blog in order to keep up with what you are doing professionally. They will see this as a useful tool to know when you might be over-loaded with work and unable to get something done on short notice. Plus if you ever plan on running a promotional sale, this is a great way to get the word out!

Posting on blogs and forums that are relevant to the services you offer is also a great way to get the word out about your business. Chatting on forums is a great way to get the "inside scoop" on your industry and in most forums you are allowed links in your profile and signature. This is a great place to put links to your blog and business pages.

Impress people on those sites with your knowledge and they are sure to check out your pages. This is also where many people will search for freelancers as well, so make sure you don't "talk the talk if you can't walk the walk".

You can even find success in posting ads on Craigslist. It may seem unconventional, but posting an ad in the "services offered" section of Craigslist can be an excellent way to bring traffic to your gig! Just be sure to put in the ad that all communications about these gig's need to be made through Fiverr. If they ignore this and e-mail you directly anyway – redirect them to your Fiverr page, ask them to create a free account and message you there.

As well as traditional social media promotion, Fiverr also offers the ability to advertise on the Fiverr forum. There is an entire board dedicated to promoting your gigs on Fiverr titled "My Fiverr Gigs". This is the ONLY section of the forum that is to be used for self-promotion. Spamming threads with your advertisements can get you in trouble, so be sure to post in the right spot!

No matter if you choose one or all of these forms of self-promotion, they are all sure fire to boost traffic to your gigs. The more options you have at your disposal, the more traffic you're going to get at your Gigs. The more traffic you can get at your Gigs, the more customers you going to have, which will result in more income for you. So, what are you waiting for? It's time to start promoting!

Actions from this chapter

- Create at least one social media stream where you can promote your gigs – Create a blog, Facebook page, Youtube channel or Twitter page.

- Promote at least one of your gigs on the Fiverr Forum.

TOP TIPS TO BECOMING A TOP RATED SELLER

If you've taken the action points at the end of each chapter, you should now be on your way to Fiverr Success. What is success to you? Only you will know that for sure, but for many people Fiverr Success is all about becoming a Top Rated Seller.

All the Top Rated Sellers on Fiverr have things in common, but the biggest and most important thing that they all share is excellent customer service.

No matter what services you choose to offer, you absolutely cannot become a Top Rated Seller if you do not provide high quality customer service along with your high quality service.

Here are some of the "Top Tips" that will lead you to become one of Fiverr's Top Rated Sellers and maybe even get featured in a Super Seller blog post on the Fiverr blog. Now that's promotion!

- o If a customer gives you their name, use it! Customers love feeling their experience is personalized when they work with a seller. A great seller knows how to sound semi-formal and human during message correspondence.

- o Get all your orders in on time! (The earlier the better!) A customer is always happy when they get their order sooner than expected. Don't mistake this for a lack of quality. Provide both.

- o Be active in the forums. Take a leadership type role helping out new sellers once you know the ropes. This is a great way to be involved in the community, get word out about your gigs as well as be seen by the Fiverr staff who handpicks the Top Rated Sellers.

o Be consistent! Always bring your best work to the table, do not deliver something you would not like to receive if you were the buyer. Be polite and communicative.

Really, there is not formula to become a Top Rated Seller. As stated earlier this rank is not an electronic promotion like the other levels. The Fiverr staff really do keep a look out and they do their best to make sure that those who deserve Top Rated Seller get it.

There is no "minimum" amount of time you have to have your account or number of sales you have to surpass in order to become a Top Rated Seller. If you talk to anyone on the forum you will find the same answers. Just do your best, work hard and be consistent. In the end, you will be rewarded for your hard work!

Actions from this chapter

- Use a customer's name on the next Gig you do. Make a point of being friendly but professional.

- Complete your next Gig at least a day early without compromising quality. Can you turn it around in half the time you stated and keep the quality high?

- Help out at least 3 new sellers on Fiverr. This will start the momentum for you. You need to be seen as a leader to become a Top Rated Seller. It's also great for your self-esteem and confidence to help other people out.

HOW TO AVOID AND OVERCOME NEGATIVE FEEDBACK

No matter if your account is brand new or has been around for years, you are going to run into a bad buyer every now and again. Earlier we mentioned how some people may ask for an insane amount of work for the price or may leave a negative review for no reason. Here are a few ways to approach these situations should they arise.

One of the biggest problems for sellers on Fiverr is when people disregard their ability to message the seller prior to ordering. In many cases, buyers have expected that the seller would be able to complete a task for them but never considered actually asking them if they could.

For example, you may offer resume services. Unfortunately, you have no experience with Photoshop (or simply do not own Photoshop) and someone wants you to use a Photoshop template to design the resume. This could end up being a big problem later on, especially if they do not mention this upfront.

Say you deliver a spectacular resume, in .PDF form. Sadly, because it is not a graphic template, your buyer is unsatisfied and leaves you a 3.5 star rating and a review that says, "Great work."

Now you are faced with a problem, you delivered your work as described (no mention of a Photoshop designed resume in your gig description) but you received a poor rating because of this. If you do not have a ton of orders completed at this point, your overall positive rating has probably dropped a percentage or two as well.

In this sort of situation it is best for you to ask the buyer if there is any way you can change their mind on the rating. If they will take the offer of a gig extra for free, in order to change it to a 5 star rating, it is totally worth it. After all, your rating is a big part of bringing in new buyers and if you can convince your buyer to change their mind you should!

If this option does not pull through, then there is always the option to dispute the review. Bringing in the Fiverr support team can help you get a bad review removed or changed. This should always be a last choice option though, always be professional and try to work things out with your buyer directly.

Perhaps though, if the person mentioned right off the bat that they are looking for a Photoshop template design then you could have gone a different route. There is always an option to mutually cancel a gig (prior to delivery). If you know you cannot deliver what the buyer is looking for, rather than risking a bad review, you are often better off with mutual cancellation.

While you do not want to have a bunch of cancellations, you are still better off. Letting the buyer cancel on you later allows them to leave a bad review anyway. With a mutual cancellation, it will not count against your positive rating. Be aware that a high number of cancellation will impact your chances of becoming a Top Rated Seller.

Trying to work around these bad buyers can be challenging at times. Also if you ever hit a slump and have trouble keeping up, your negative review might actually be your fault. When you know you are at fault for a bad review you can still attempt to make it up to your buyer and change their mind. If they do not go for the idea though, you just have to keep moving forward.

If you ever find yourself in a situation like this, then really you just have to accept it and move on. Make sure that you stay on the ball with all your future orders. This is the only way to come back from negative feedback. If you find that you fell into a slump, try figuring out why and working towards making sure it never happens again. Does your Gig description or Profile need to be clearer? Can you communicate in a way that's friendlier and less confrontational?

As long as you keep it up, you can bring any rating back up to at least 99%, even if it takes a while. You just have to keep your dream alive and keep working towards that goal of becoming a Top Rated Seller. Don't let one or two bad experiences keep you from reaching your potential.

Prevention is better than cure. If you're able to set up an accurate Profile/Gig description, keep communication regular, friendly and positive, and deliver on what you're saying you're going to do - it will all work towards positive feedback and hopefully you won't need to count on this chapter.

Actions from this chapter

- Look back over your Gig Descriptions and Profile. Are they correct and accurate? Could you be more specific on what you offer to meet the customer's expectations?

- If you get an unsatisfied customer – Apologize quickly and authentically. Offer a free gig extra and ask how you can help them reconsider their rating.

- If you receive negative feedback, and they won't reconsider – Focus on completing at least 20 more Gigs with a 100% success rate. This will mean their feedback is less than 5% of your total score, and less influential to future customers.

CAN FIVERR REALLY PAY MY BILLS AND MORE?

To put it simply, yes. Fiverr can absolutely replace your salary and maybe then some! It really depends all on how much time, effort and care you put into your business on Fiverr. Those who thrive are usually the ones who have a purpose and a goal or the people who really have a passion for what they do and love doing it. The ultimate combination is having both!

Choosing a gig to sell on Fiverr is easy for some and difficult for others. You can consider things that are obviously profitable like graphic or web design, but you could also offer simple services that you just enjoy providing. Some of the services offered on Fiverr may seem a little ridiculous, but in the end, someone is doing what they love to do and getting paid for it. That is the one of the best feelings that anyone can imagine.

When you want to become a Top Rated Seller and replace your day job with Fiverr gigs, make that your goal from the get-go. If you want to see it work out then you have to put in the effort to make it happen. You cannot simply expect that it is going to just happen magically, because it doesn't. Have you taken the steps at the end of each chapter?!

There are several people who work only on Fiverr and make a great living off of it. They all have repeat business and offer the same great quality again and again.

One of the biggest things these people have accomplished, is that they sell more gigs with extra's than without. Also, they price their extras competitively but they also do not do more work than they should for a certain amount. Hey have the right balance. Often, things like this are learned over time and by looking at gigs similar to your own to see what the going-rates are.

Above all, do not get discouraged! Some people never accomplish more than a little extra spending money with their Fiverr account. Of course, most of these people already have a job they love and were only looking for extra money. This is not a bad thing – when those people get over loaded they will pass on jobs to those who do intend to generate a full-time income on Fiverr.

In the end it is time and patience that will pay off the most. The harder you work at promoting, ensuring the best customer care possible and always deliver a superior service, people are bound to come back to you again and again.

Actions from this chapter

- Have you achieved the goals you set in Chapter 1?

- Write a strong, personal reason <u>why</u> you want to achieve that goal. Do you want to leave your 9-5 job? Do you want to buy a particular car or fund the holiday of a lifetime? It's so important to consider the why behind any goal.

FIVERR SUCCESSES AND SUPER SELLERS

Just about everyone on Fiverr has read a Super Seller blog post at least once. These sellers are chosen by Fiverr staff not only to become a Top Rated Seller but also to be featured in the blog as Super Sellers. Most if not all of these people have become full-time Fiverr's as well as have accomplished a string of goals they thought would be impossible before they discovered Fiverr.

One of the most recognizable of all the Fiverr Super Sellers goes by the username Madmoo. She started out testing the waters with no real goal in mind – until that first sale came in. For a lot of sellers, this is what drives them and for Madmoo especially. She seems to be motivated by every bit of positive feedback she receives and relies 100% on quality in customer care and services provided to get such wonderful feedback.

"I find it hard to see myself as successful. It's one reason I love getting feedback – when someone appreciates what I did and tells me I'm wonderful or awesome, it makes me smile." –Madmoo, Fiverr Super Seller Blog Post. - See more at: http://blog.fiverr.com/madmoo-youre-a-fiverr-superseller/#sthash.GgmnIFC0.dpuf

Madmoo went from working full-time in a call center with a side-income through Fiverr until she was given the opportunity to work part-time at her day job. Not long after that, her ability to give more time to her Fiverr business had increased her sales to the point where she was eventually able to make a full-time income through Fiverr!

Do you like the idea of giving up your day job and working for yourself on Fiverr full time? It's a possibility and it's down to you!

Another Super Seller who has accomplished great things on Fiverr goes by the user name chrishardy. This Super Seller heard about Fiverr on the Clark Howard show which is when he made the decision to offer voice over services on Fiverr.

Since joining Fiverr, Chris was able to use his vocal talents to not only create a side income, but actually replace his corporate job. Chris and his wife moved and instead of looking for a new corporate job he and his wife now work part-time as independent contractors, allowing them to live their lives as they please.

"Fiverr has also been great for my self-esteem. I get tons of positive feedback from the community, which makes me feel really good about myself, and at the same time I'm making money to pay bills." – chrishardy, Fiverr Super Seller Blog Post - See more at: http://blog.fiverr.com/chris-hardy-super-seller-fiverr-star/#sthash.0Y6JniyD.dpuf

The last Super Seller we will mention here is Bookreviewstew. This seller is actually an actor from LA who had small roles in movies like Mr. and Mrs. Smith, Collateral and The Shaggy Dog just to name a few. One day he and his wife decided that LA was not the place for their family and they moved to Colorado.

With that decision, working in big movie productions were out of the picture, but Fiverr now makes up around 60% of his income. While he is not full-time on Fiverr, this seller couldn't be happier with their business.

"For me personally, I'd rather give them back their money over getting a bad review." – Bookreviewstew Fiverr Super Sellers Blog - See more at: http://blog.fiverr.com/actor-making-money-online/#sthash.ukSOPJ70.dpuf

All these success stories have a couple of things in common:

- o They love what they do

- o They are motivated by positive feedback

- o They focus on quality communication and service

If these success stories were not enough to prove to you that Fiverr is a worthwhile way to generate a side income that can be built up into a full-time income, then visit the Fiverr Blog to read more Super Seller stories!

These stories are proof that anyone with the right mindset can make a full time living on Fiverr. Use these stories as inspiration to expand your skills and Gig deliveries.

Actions from this chapter

- Read at least one of the Super Seller Stories above.

- Go onto the Fiverr Blog and find another Super Seller story of your choosing.

Make a mental note that if you're ever doubting whether you can make a success on Fiver in the future - to read at least one Super Seller story on Fiverr to boost your confidence and belief once more.

CONCLUSION

Fiverr is a great opportunity for anyone looking to generate an income, no matter how small or how large. If you can see it in your own mind, then it can become a reality.

Yes, you will still have a few annoying customers here and there, but that will happen anywhere you go, no matter what industry you are in. Over all though, most of the customers you will get on Fiverr are really looking for a great service at a great price. If you can provide them that along with great customer service and an exceptional final product, most buyers will leave you an outstanding review!

Yes, this does require actual work! The thing about this is, with Fiverr, you can choose whatever you want for your gig. So make sure it is something you love! If you choose something that you know you are good at, but you don't really like, it will still feel like work and you're less likely to stick to it.

If you can find a niche that you absolutely, truly, love, then you will be successful no matter what. When you are doing something you enjoy, even if it is hard work, it will no longer feel like it. That is the biggest key to success on Fiverr.

Anyone can sell a service for $5 and make a profit, but only Super Sellers can create a career they love with services starting at $5!

OTHER BOOKS BY BRAD JONES

Ebay Excellence: Making Easy Money The Ebay Way

Blogging Brilliance: How To Make A Bundle On Your Blog

Flawless Freelance Writing: How To Make A Fortune Freelance Writing